GOD'S
Healing Redemption
for You and for Me

Biblical References from Genesis Through Revelation

Healing from the Father Through the Son By the Holy Spirit

A Compilation with Comments by father Boyd

God's Healing Redemption Promises
Explanations of Key Scripture Verses from Genesis to Revelation

All illustrations used by permission from Free Bible Images and Sweet Publishing.

Visit http://theredemptionstory.org to download a copy of these publications and lessons.

This is a free publication, but if you would like to consider making a donation to further the outreach of this message, please visit http://newharvest.org.

Cover Design and Editorial Work by Linda Stubblefield, Arrow Computer Services

"Give ear, O heavens, and I will speak; And hear, O earth, the words of my mouth. Let my teaching drop as the rain, My speech distill as the dew, As raindrops on the tender herb, And as showers on the grass. For I proclaim the name of the LORD: Ascribe greatness to our God."

(Deuteronomy 32:1-3)

"Eye has not seen, nor ear heard, Nor have entered into the heart of man The things which God has prepared for those who love Him."

(I Corinthians 2:9)

Scripture questions may be directed to the following email address:
bberends1238@gmail.com

The Biblical Scripture references in this book show the healing power of God through His Son, Jesus Christ, from Genesis through Revelation. The texts used are taken from the New King James Version of the Holy Scriptures, and the reader is encouraged to compare the Biblical texts in other versions.

> All Scriptures point to God as the Healer of mankind and is carried out today through His Son, Jesus Christ, both as prophesied and as promised in the Bible.

Mankind was created healthy, but sin separated man from God spiritually, and sin also caused the separation from the perfect health given by God at Creation.

> But God had a backup plan, and Satan was unaware of God's "Plan B." God sent His Son, Jesus Christ, not only to die for our sins, but to offer a restored health from sickness, diseases, addictions, mental problems, and ruined relationships.

Just as eternal life is yours for the asking, even so restoration from all manner of sickness and disease is also yours for the asking. Neither gift is automatic; each must be requested.

> Salvation and healing are not a package deal. Both salvation and healing must, by faith, be requested, claimed, and received separately.

As you read these Scripture verses in this small guide, ask the Holy Spirit to guide you into all of the Biblical truth and understanding found in these inspired verses.

God Created the Earth

Genesis 1:1, *"In the beginning God created the heavens and the earth."*

God created man (Adam) and woman (Eve).

Man sinned in the garden.

God promised to redeem mankind.

"In the beginning God created the heavens and the earth. The earth was without form, and void; and darkness was on the face of the deep. And the Spirit of God was hovering over the face of the waters." (Genesis 1:1, 2)

"And the LORD God formed man of the dust of the ground, and breathed into his nostrils the breath of life; and man became a living being. ¹And the LORD God caused a deep sleep to fall on Adam, and he slept; and He took one of his ribs, and closed up the flesh in its place. Then the rib which the LORD God had taken from man He made into a woman, and He brought her to the man." (Genesis 2:7, 21, 22)

Some have said that these two words—"God created"—are the two most important in the entire Bible. If you can believe that God created everything out of the words of His mouth "by faith," then you can believe the rest of the Bible. When it happened or how Creation occurred isn't important. The key point is that God created all things.

The creation story continues with the creation of Adam and Eve. God had now given man everything he needed with a place to live and a woman to live with him.

However, God had also given to mankind a free will to obey or disobey God. God created man to love and obey Him, but God wanted a real relationship with mankind. Therefore, He gave man the freedom to choose.

– father Boyd

Then the serpent said to the woman, "You will not surely die. For God knows that in the day you eat of it your eyes will be opened, and you will be like God, knowing good and evil." So when the woman saw that the tree was good for food, that it was pleasant to the eyes, and a tree desirable to make one wise, she took of its fruit and ate. She also gave to her husband with her, and he ate. (Genesis 3:4-6)

On that sad and tragic day when man decided to disobey God, sin entered into the world. Because of the entrance of sin and sickness into God's perfect creation, He had to initiate His plan and promise of redemption from sin and restoration from all sickness and disease. This plan eventually led to the restoration and forgiveness of all mankind through the sacrifice and death of Jesus Christ on the Cross. And it was through this plan of redemption for sin that Father God, through the suffering and humiliation of Jesus at Calvary, also made provision for restoration to full health—body, mind, and spirit.

– father Boyd

2

God Destroys Mankind; Noah Finds Grace!

Genesis 6:5, *"Then the LORD saw that the wickedness of man was great in the earth, and that every intent of the thoughts of his heart was only evil continually."*

God flooded the earth and saved eight.

God called a nation through Abraham.

Abraham believed God—the first healing.

And the LORD was sorry that He had made man on the earth, and He was grieved in His heart. So the LORD said, "I will destroy man whom I have created from the face of the earth, both man and beast, creeping thing and birds of the air, for I am sorry that I have made them." But Noah found grace in the eyes of the LORD. (Genesis 6:6-8)

Adam and Eve had many children, and the world's population continued to grow. In time, mankind consistently chose sin over obeying God, and the evil on the earth continued to grow worse. God's promise of redemption was made in the garden of Eden, but in order for this promise to be fulfilled toward mankind, someone had to survive the great flood that was coming.

– father Boyd

"And behold, I Myself am bringing floodwaters on the earth, to destroy from under heaven all flesh in which is the breath of life; everything that is on the earth shall die. But I will establish My covenant with you; and you shall go into the ark—you, your sons, your wife, and your sons' wives with you." (Genesis 6:17, 18)

In this new, small beginning, God re-established His promise of redemption and covenant through Noah and his sons. God spared Noah and his family—Shem, Ham, and Japheth and their wives. They lived long lives and repopulated the earth. But as the world's population increased and evil and sin also began to increase, sickness and disease also re-entered. But God's promise to send a Redeemer was yet to be fulfilled. God would need someone He could trust to follow His plan and promise. From the family of Noah, God decided that His Son, Jesus Christ, would one day come to fulfill His plan of salvation and restoration of healing through the lineage of Shem. Jesus, through His death, redeemed mankind from their sins, and with the stripes that Jesus bore on His back, He redeemed us from sickness and disease.

– father Boyd

Now the LORD had said to Abram: "Get out of your country, From your family and from your father's house, To a land that I will show you. I will make you a great nation; I will bless you and make your name great; And you shall be a blessing. I will bless those who bless you, And I will curse him who curses you; And in you all the families of the earth shall be blessed." (Genesis 12:1-4)

Noah, Shem, and then Abram heard and listened to the call of God. As a result of their obedience and God's grace, the promise of redemption from sin and the restoration of man's health continues today to all who will trust God and believe by faith in the promises from Father God, which were fulfilled through His Son, Jesus Christ! Will you, by faith, believe His promises to remove your sins from His sight and allow Jesus Christ not only to save you for all eternity, but to provide you with health and healing in this life?

– father Boyd

2a — God Never Forgets What He Has Promised.

Genesis 17:1, 2, When Abram was ninety-nine years old, the LORD appeared to Abram and said to him, "I am Almighty God; walk before Me and be blameless. And I will make My covenant between Me and you, and will multiply you exceedingly."

"And he believed in the LORD, and He accounted it to him for righteousness." (Genesis 15:6)

"Is anything too hard for the LORD?…" (Genesis 30:22)

The birth of the promised son Isaac from a 100-year-old father and a 90-year-old mother was definitely a God-given miracle. Both Abraham and Sarah had to believe and trust God for a long time before Father God delivered on His promise. Because Abram believed and trusted God without ever seeing any results, God accounted his faith as righteousness.

How long are you willing to believe and trust the Lord to reward your faith and trust?

– father Boyd

"Then God remembered Rachel, and God listened to her and opened her womb." (Genesis 30:22)

"So you shall serve the LORD your God, and He will bless your bread and your water. And I will take sickness away from the midst of you. No one shall suffer miscarriage or be barren in your land; I will fulfill the number of your days." (Exodus 23:25, 26)

…"If you diligently heed the voice of the LORD your God and do what is right in His sight, give ear to His commandments and keep all His statutes, I will put none of the diseases on you which I have brought on the Egyptians. For I am the LORD who heals you." (Exodus 15:26)

Father God was already active in the earliest parts of the Bible, not only in healing, opening up wombs (which is healing), rewarding faith, and asking if anything was too hard for Him to accomplish.

God promises to reward your faith and trust in Him based upon what He is able to do. Remember, in Genesis 30 He asked if there was anything too hard for Him to do. He went on to say that a person's very faith and trust in Him is what He would consider righteous in His eyes.

Yes, God provided miracles, but He promised to do even more than that. If you are willing to trust Him, He would also keep sickness and disease from happening to you.

God has promised through His Son, Jesus Christ, to redeem us from our sins and give us eternal life. But we do not receive the full benefits of eternal life until we die. Through Jesus Christ, we have also been redeemed from sickness and diseases. We can enjoy that part of the redemption process on earth before we die!

If you will only trust Him, God is offering you so much while requiring so little of you in exchange.

Father God is willing to heal you if you are willing to have the faith to trust Him. But He doesn't stop there; He is willing to see that you have the faith necessary through His Holy Spirit. All you have to do is ask for it.

– father Boyd

3 The Bible's First Recorded Miracles

Genesis 20:17, "So Abraham prayed to God; and God healed Abimelech, his wife, and his female servants. Then they bore children."

The choice was to believe or to doubt.

God promised and delivered a miracle.

God performed what He promised!

"And the LORD visited Sarah as He had said, and the LORD did for Sarah as He had spoken. For Sarah conceived and bore Abraham a son in his old age, at the set time of which God had spoken to him. And Abraham called the name of his son who was born to him—whom Sarah bore to him—Isaac. Then Abraham circumcised his son Isaac when he was eight days old, as God had commanded him. Now Abraham was one hundred years old when his son Isaac was born to him." (Genesis 21:1-5)

Note that the first two miracles recorded in the Bible dealt with having children. In God's eyes, children are very important. God has never changed, so His children can ask Him for a child, and He will hear and answer.

Remember, Abraham never quite believed—even as the promise appeared to have disappeared.

– father Boyd

The New Is in the Old Contained;
The Old Is in the New Explained.

God told Abram to leave Ur of the Chaldees.

Abram obeyed God.

Abram built an altar to worship.

"And he believed in the LORD, and He [God] accounted it to him for righteousness." (Genesis 15:6)

"Is anything too hard for the LORD?…" (Genesis 18:14)

"Then God remembered Rachel, and God listened to her and opened her womb." (Genesis 30:22)

…there He [God] tested them, and said, "If you diligently heed the voice of the LORD your God and do what is right in His sight, give ear to His commandments and keep all His statutes, I will put none of the diseases on you which I have brought on the Egyptians. For I am the LORD who heals you." (Exodus 15:25, 26)

"So you shall serve the LORD your God, and He will bless your bread and your water. And I will take sickness away from the midst of you. No one shall suffer miscarriage or be barren in your land; I will fulfill the number of your days. (Exodus 23:25, 26)

Note that what God considers righteous in His eyes is your faith. And then He reminds us that nothing is too hard for Him (Genesis 15:6, 18:14).

God's third recorded healing also involved having a child, but only after Rachel had prayed for a long time. God listens to His children, and out of His great love, He provides.

Father God also promises that if you will listen to Him and believe that He is God for whom nothing is impossible, He will keep you healthy. He will do so by blessing what you eat and drink, and He will also give you a long life (Exodus 15:26, 23:25, 26).

- father Boyd

Look, Believe, and Live!

Deuteronomy 7:6, *"For you are a holy people to the Lord your God; the Lord your God has chosen you to be a people for Himself, a special treasure…"*

Miracles are not all physical in nature.

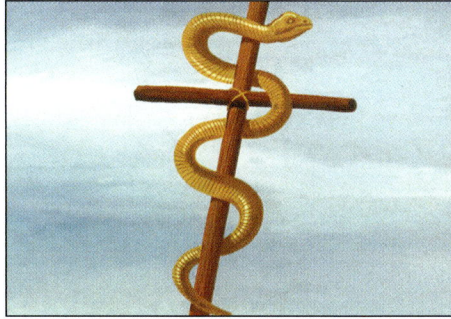
God provided a way.

"Look, believe, and live!"

And the people spoke against God and against Moses: "Why have you brought us up out of Egypt to die in the wilderness? For there is no food and no water, and our soul loathes this worthless bread." So the LORD sent fiery serpents among the people, and they bit the people; and many of the people of Israel died.

Therefore the people came to Moses, and said, "We have sinned, for we have spoken against the LORD and against you; pray to the LORD that He take away the serpents from us." So Moses prayed for the people.

Then the LORD said to Moses, "Make a fiery serpent, and set it on a pole; and it shall be that everyone who is bitten, when he looks at it, shall live." So Moses made a bronze serpent, and put it on a pole; and so it was, if a serpent had bitten anyone, when he looked at the bronze serpent, he lived. (Numbers 21:5-9)

Father God brought His people out of captivity— like Jesus brought us out from sin and from sickness. God was meeting the Hebrew children's needs by feeding them and providing them with water to drink. Instead of being thankful, the people of God complained incessantly.

First, God punished them with fiery serpents; then in His grace and mercy, He forgave them and saved them. In this case, the healing from death was accomplished through Moses' intercessory prayer.

– father Boyd

God Never Changes—
He Healed, He Heals, and He Will Heal You.

Moses passed the mantle to Joshua.

Moses recorded God's Laws.

Moses looked on the Promised Land.

"For you are a holy people to the LORD your God; the LORD your God has chosen you to be a people for Himself, a special treasure above all the peoples on the face of the earth." (Deuteronomy 7:6)

"Moses was one hundred and twenty years old when he died. His eyes were not dim nor his natural vigor diminished." (Deuteronomy 34:7)

"And the LORD will take away from you all sickness, and will afflict you with none of the terrible diseases of Egypt which you have known, but will lay them on all those who hate you." (Deuteronomy 7:15)

In Deuteronomy 7:6, Father God tells His children exactly how special they are to Him. Moses was so special that God never put the failings of old age on him. Deuteronomy 34:7 says Moses' eyesight was not diminished; in other words, he didn't need glasses! He enjoyed the natural vigor of a young man.

In fact, in Deuteronomy 7:15, God promised to keep sickness and disease from His children. As God is no respecter of persons, that promise also includes you—if you will put Him first in your life and trust Him.

– father Boyd

Hannah Prayed in Desperation;
Elisha Prayed in Faith…and God Heard Them.

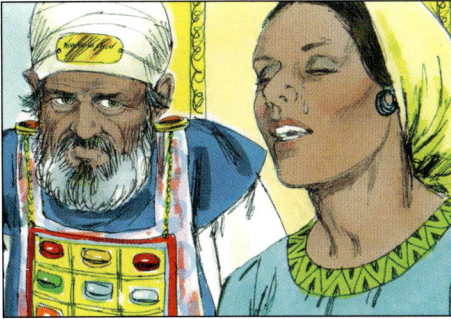

Eli thought Hannah was drunk.

God knew better!

Is anything too hard for God?

Then Eli answered and said, "Go in peace, and the God of Israel grant your petition which you have asked of Him.…" So it came to pass in the process of time that Hannah conceived and bore a son, and called his name Samuel, saying, "Because I have asked for him from the LORD." (I Samuel 1:17, 20)

When Elisha came into the house, there was the child, lying dead on his bed. He went in therefore, shut the door behind the two of them, and prayed to the LORD. And he went up and lay on the child, and put his mouth on his mouth, his eyes on his eyes, and his hands on his hands; and he stretched himself out on the child, and the flesh of the child became warm. He returned and walked back and forth in the house, and again went up and stretched himself out on him; then the child sneezed seven times, and the child opened his eyes. And he called Gehazi and said, "Call this Shunammite woman." So he called her. And when she came in to him, he said, "Pick up your son." (II Kings 4:32-36)

Hannah knew her only hope for a child was through a miracle from God.

If your only hope for healing is from God, then pray as Hannah did. Pour out your heart to Him, and then trust Him for your miracle.

Elisha knew that a miracle was needed and only his God could supply. Elisha prayed until God answered.

God will hear your prayers and will answer if you will put your trust in Him. Pray and believe until He gives you your answer.

– father Boyd

6

God Heals an Unbelieving Gentile.
God Also Heals Through Fervent Prayer.

Naaman, a man of valor, was a leper.

Naaman washed and became clean.

Hezekiah asked for healing.

Now Naaman, commander of the army of the king of Syria, was a great and honorable man in the eyes of his master, because by him the LORD had given victory to Syria. He was also a mighty man of valor, but a leper.... And Elisha sent a messenger to him, saying, "Go and wash in the Jordan seven times, and your flesh shall be restored to you, and you shall be clean." (II Kings 5:1, 10)

In those days Hezekiah was sick and near death. And Isaiah the prophet, the son of Amoz, went to him and said to him, "Thus says the LORD: 'Set your house in order, for you shall die, and not live.'" Then he turned his face toward the wall, and prayed to the LORD, saying, "Remember now, O LORD, I pray, how I have walked before You in truth and with a loyal heart, and have done what was good in Your sight." And Hezekiah wept bitterly. And it happened, before Isaiah had gone out into the middle court, that the word of the LORD came to him, saying, "Return and tell Hezekiah the leader of My people, 'Thus says the LORD, the God of David your father: "I have heard your prayer, I have seen your tears; surely I will heal you. On the third day you shall go up to the house of the LORD. And I will add to your days fifteen years. I will deliver you and this city from the hand of the king of Assyria; and I will defend this city for My own sake, and for the sake of My servant David." Then Isaiah said, "Take a lump of figs." So they took and laid it on the boil, and he recovered. (II Kings 20:1-7)

Naaman was not an Israelite; rather, he was one of the hated Gentiles. He did not have faith when his Israelite slave girl told him about a man of God who could heal him of his leprosy. Though he was skeptical, he figured, "What have I got to lose?" So he went to Israel to seek the prophet. However, when Elisha sent a message instead of meeting him in person, Naaman's pride almost kept him from being healed.

Pride creates doubt that keeps God from providing a person's healing. When God directs, do not argue! Listen and then do it His way.

Hezekiah was a king who, to the best of his ability, served and trusted God. However, He still became sick. God didn't mess around and sent a prophet to tell him that he was not going to get better.

When you get a bad word or a sickness, etc., that you don't think you deserve, you too can do what Hezekiah did and go directly to God. Tell Him why you do not deserve whatever has come upon you. God is no respecter of persons, and He will listen. In Hezekiah's case, God not only restored him to health, but God gave Hezekiah fifteen more years to live.

God hears, God answers, and God is generous.

– father Boyd

7

Father God Promises, Father God Puts It in Writing, Then Father God Delivers.

The Lord also promises He will personally get involved in our healing.

"I have heard your prayers, and I have seen your tears. I will heal you." – God

---

"Because you have made the LORD, who is my refuge, even the Most High, your dwelling place, No evil shall befall you, Nor shall any plague come near your dwelling; For He shall give His angels charge over you, to keep you in all your ways." (Psalm 91:9-11)

"Bless the LORD, O my soul, and forget not all His benefits: Who forgives all your iniquities, who heals all your diseases." (Psalm 103:2, 3)

"The LORD is near to all who call upon Him, to all who call upon Him in truth. He will fulfill the desire of those who fear Him; He also will hear their cry and save them." (Psalm 145:18, 19)

"Have mercy on me, O LORD, for I am weak; O LORD, heal me, for my bones [body] are troubled.…The LORD has heard my supplication [prayers]; the LORD will receive my prayer." (Psalm 6:2, 9)

"The LORD opens the eyes of the blind; The LORD raises those who are bowed down; The LORD loves the righteous." (Psalm 146:8)

"He heals the brokenhearted and binds up their wounds." (Psalm 147:3)

In these verses, God is speaking to those who have made Him Lord of their life. He promises that no evil or sickness will come near them, and He places angels in charge to see that His promises are kept.

God reminds us not to forget all the benefits He will provide, including protection, healing, and everything else. However, we need to faithfully pray, believe, and trust Him with all of our being.

The psalmist is aware of exactly how weak he really is, and his only hope is that God will have mercy on him. Sickness is upon him, and his only hope is that the Lord will hear his prayer.

What does our Lord promise? He will heal the blind, and if sickness has weighed you down, He will raise you up. He will heal more than physical sickness. He is better than bandages when He heals, and He loves those who love Him.

– father Boyd

These all cried out to God, and He heard them all.

"O LORD my God, I cried out to You, and You healed me." (Psalm 30:2)

"In my distress I called upon the LORD, and cried out to my God; He heard my voice from His temple, and my cry came before Him, even to His ears." (Psalm 18:6)

"I sought the LORD, and He heard me, and delivered me from all my fears." (Psalm 34:4)

"Then they cried out to the LORD in their trouble, and He delivered them out of their distresses....He sent His word and healed them, and delivered them from their destructions." (Psalm 107:6, 20)

God often puts your trust in Him, as well as your faith in Him, to the test. However, He will always hear your cry, and all of your prayers will always come before Him.

The sweet psalmist of Israel was often referred to as "a man after God's own heart." Yet the man often endured problems with his health, often suffered from depression, and often sinned against God. Still the psalmist never doubted that God would not only forgive, but that God would also restore.

When the psalmist had problems or suffered from sickness of any kind, he always went to God and shared his fears. I am sure that sometimes he even had doubts that he shared, and I am sure that God always delivered.

Psalm 107 is prophetic. The psalmist is writing to you and to me. If we will cry out to our Lord in our trouble, which is what sickness can be, God will deliver us.

This prophetic chapter goes beyond simply a promise. God goes so far as to tell us He would send Jesus to heal us and deliver us from all destructions or sickness or disease.

– father Boyd

Solomon received wisdom from God to administer justice.

"Trust in the LORD with all your heart, and lean not on your own understanding; In all your ways acknowledge Him, And He shall direct your paths. Do not be wise in your own eyes; Fear the LORD and depart from evil. It will be health to your flesh, And strength to your bones." (Proverbs 3:5-8)

Solomon was considered the wisest man who ever lived, and what he shared with the two women who were fighting over a baby is probably one of the wisest decisions that a mortal man has ever decreed.

Solomon, at least early on in his rule, trusted God with all of his heart, and he relied on God for making decisions in difficult situations. As long as he did not trust in his own wisdom, he was never wrong in his judgments. Solomon trusted God in everything he did, and God was faithful to direct him in all that he did.

Solomon shared with us that if we would not consider our own wisdom and trust the Lord, then the Lord would keep us from doing evil. If we placed our trust in Him, it would be health to our bodies and strength to our bones.

– father Boyd

Prayer to God Will Bring Wisdom.

Availing himself of God's wisdom helped Solomon to make the right decision.

"There is a way that seems right to a man, but its end is the way of death." (Proverbs 14:12)

"For they are life to those who find them, and health to all their flesh." (Proverbs 4:22)

"The fear of the LORD prolongs days, but the years of the wicked will be shortened." (Proverbs 10:27)

"A sound heart is life to the body, but envy is rottenness to the bones." (Proverbs 14:30)

"Pleasant words are like a honeycomb, Sweetness to the soul and health to the bones." (Proverbs 16:24)

"Do not be wise in your own eyes; fear the LORD and depart from evil. It will be health to your flesh, and strength to your bones." (Proverbs 3:7, 8)

"The light of the eyes rejoices the heart, and a good report makes the bones healthy." (Proverbs 15:30)

"My son, do not forget my law, but let your heart keep my commands; For length of days and long life and peace they will add to you." (Proverbs 3:1, 2)

Solomon was wise enough to know that his wisdom would lead to his death, but God's wisdom would provide life.

Solomon shared God's wisdom—that His words led not only to life, but to complete health as well as long life.

Pleasant words are sweet not only to your soul but to the soul of another. In addition, plesant words are a benefit to health; however, if anyone is envious, it will lead to sickness of the body.

Once again Solomon tells us not to think we are wise on our own. True wisdom is to fear the Lord (in the right way) and leave evil behind.

If the Lord is the light of our eyes, the promise is that He will give us health, make our bones strong, and give us long life as well as provide peace for all of those days.

There is a condition, however. You must listen and serve the Lord.

– father Boyd

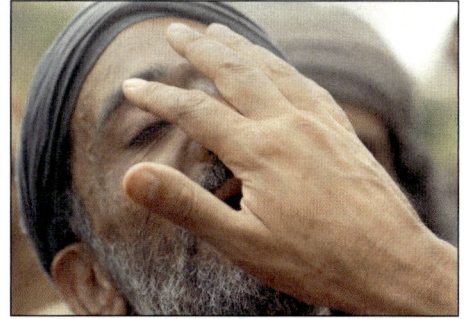

All of the healing Isaiah said Jesus would do, He did.

"Then the eyes of the blind shall be opened, and the ears of the deaf shall be unstopped. Then the lame shall leap like a deer, and the tongue of the dumb sing." (Isaiah 35:5, 6)

"But those who wait on the LORD shall renew their strength; They shall mount up with wings like eagles, They shall run and not be weary, They shall walk and not faint." (Isaiah 40:31)

"I, the LORD, have called You in righteousness, and will hold Your hand; I will keep You and give You as a covenant to the people, as a light to the Gentiles, To open blind eyes, to bring out prisoners from the prison, Those who sit in darkness from the prison house. I am the LORD, that is My name; and My glory I will not give to another, Nor My praise to carved images." (Isaiah 42:6-8)

Isaiah the prophet lived a considerable length of time before Jesus Christ came to the earth. But God used Isaiah to tell the future generations about the Son of God who was coming to redeem His children from their sins and to restore health and healing into their lives.

Isaiah gives us God's words regarding God's Son and what Jesus will do when He comes. Jesus will open the eyes of the blind and the ears of the deaf. Those with walking difficulties will be restored to full strength, and even the dumb, or those with speech problems, will have their speech restored.

But Jesus does not stop with physical healing. Jesus restores your mind and your soul so that you will no longer be depressed, and you will not grow weary while serving Him.

Father God says that He will do all this for us, but we had better never forget that He will do this so that we will give Him the glory and not give the glory to anyone else.

- father Boyd

The prophesied Christ came, died, and healed.

*Surely He has borne our griefs and carried our sorrows; Yet we esteemed Him stricken, Smitten by God, and afflicted. But He was wounded for our transgressions, He was bruised for our iniquities; The chastisement for our peace was upon Him, **and by His stripes we are healed.*** (Isaiah 53:4, 5)

*"The Spirit of the Lord GOD is upon Me, because the Lord has anointed Me to preach good tidings to the poor; He has sent Me **to heal the brokenhearted**, to proclaim liberty to the captives, and the opening of the prison to those who are bound."* (Isaiah 61:1)

"It shall come to pass that before they call, I will answer; and while they are still speaking, I will hear." (Isaiah 65:24)

Many years before God sent His Son, Jesus, to this earth that He had created, God also spoke prophetically through His servants.

Isaiah tells us why God sent Jesus to the earth. He would carry our sins as well as our sorrows—especially the sorrows caused by sickness, disease, and mental issues. Yes, Jesus Christ died for our sins so that we could be made right with God and then spend eternity with Him. But Jesus also suffered wounds and was beaten prior to His death on the Cross in order to redeem you and me in this lifetime from all the afflictions that keep us from enjoying a full, healthy, and long life.

Isaiah made very clear what God had told him to write about why Jesus was beaten so brutally: *"...and by His stripes **we are** healed."*

It was said of Jesus that He would preach *(how did Jesus teach and preach?)* to the poor, He would heal those who were in distress or with mental problems, and He would free those from being in a prison caused by His Enemy, Satan.

And Father God makes **you** a promise. He promises that He will be waiting for **your** call, and He will answer while **you** are still speaking.

Can Father God make it any clearer?

– father Boyd

God's Faithfulness Knows
No Limits and Has No Limits.

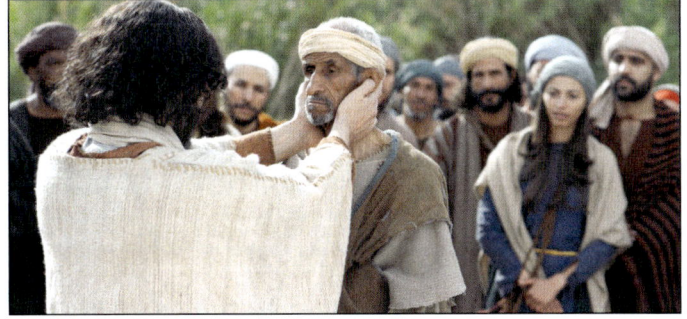

Jesus Christ brought health and healing when He became flesh and walked among us.

"For I will restore health to you and heal you of your wounds," says the LORD...." (Jeremiah 30:17)

"Behold, I will bring it health and healing; I will heal them and reveal to them the abundance of peace and truth." (Jeremiah 33:6)

"Behold, I am the LORD, the God of all flesh. Is there anything too hard for Me?" (Jeremiah 32:27)

"Call to Me, and I will answer you, and show you great and mighty things, which you do not know." (Jeremiah 33:3)

Through the LORD's mercies we are not consumed, Because His compassions fail not. They are new every morning; Great is Your faithfulness. "The LORD is my portion," says my soul, "Therefore I hope in Him!" The LORD is good to those who wait for Him, to the soul who seeks Him. It is good that one should hope and wait quietly for the salvation [and healing] of the LORD. (Lamentations 3:22-26)

Father God makes it very clear who will provide health and healing to you. Notice that God separates "health" and "healing." Obviously, if a child of God has health, he will not need healing.

But God goes beyond the simple act of healing. In the process, He will also make the believer aware of His peace and truth in abundance.

Father God makes it very clear that He is responsible for all mankind. And that, as the great God, nothing is too hard for Him to do. My friend, He will do mighty things that we do not even ask for.

Lamentations tells us that it is only because of His mercy and compassion that we are not destroyed for our sins. Every day those feelings and compassion for us are renewed because He is faithful to you and to me.

Father God also cautions His children to place their hope in Him and to wait for His goodness, salvation, and by implication, His healing.

– father Boyd

13 Eye Has Not Seen, Nor Ear Heard, Nor Have Entered Into the Heart of Man the Things Which God Has Prepared for Those Who Love Him.

Jesus healed those who sought His help; He was never a respecter of persons.

I will feed My flock, and I will make them lie down," says the Lord GOD. "I will seek what was lost and bring back what was driven away, bind up the broken and strengthen what was sick; but I will destroy the fat and the strong, and feed them in judgment." (Ezekiel 34:15, 16)

"Come, and let us return to the LORD; For He has torn, but He will heal us; He has stricken, but He will bind us up." (Hosea 6:1)

...and the God who holds your breath in His hand and owns all your ways, you have not glorified." (Daniel 5:23)

"...the people who know their God shall be strong, and carry out great exploits." (Daniel 11:32)

"My people are destroyed for lack of knowledge...." (Hosea 6:1)

The weak you have not strengthened, nor have you healed those who were sick, nor bound up the broken, nor brought back what was driven away, nor sought what was lost; but with force and cruelty you have ruled them. So they were scattered because there was no shepherd...." (Ezekiel 34:4, 5)

God Himself will take care of His people, and He will give them such peace that they will lie down and trust Him. Through His Spirit, He will seek those who are lost or driven away. He promises to heal and to strengthen those who are sick.

Father God owns us because He has made us, and God is not happy when we do not glorify Him. He invites all those whom He has punished because He wants to heal them and hold each hand. If we will place our trust in Him, He will not only make us strong, but He also wants to use us to carry out great things in His kingdom.

God also has a warning to those who hold positions of leadership and training in His kingdom on this earth. Because of some of you, Father God's people are destroyed. The rest of God's children who are considered saints in His eyes likewise have not even helped the weak, healed the sick, comforted the broken-hearted, worked to bring back those who have left the fold, and provided leadership like a shepherd does.

– father Boyd

Ezekiel spoke to the dry bones.

The frightened sailors threw Jonah overboard.

God sent a "big fish" to save Jonah.

*"To everything there is a season, A time for every purpose under heaven: A time to be born, And a time to die; A time to plant, And a time to pluck what is planted; **A time to kill** [be sick], **And a time to heal**; A time to break down, And a time to build up; A time to weep, And a time to laugh; A time to mourn, And a time to dance; A time to cast away stones, And a time to gather stones; A time to embrace, And a time to refrain from embracing; A time to gain, And a time to lose; A time to keep, And a time to throw away; A time to tear, And a time to sew; A time to keep silence, And a time to speak; A time to love, And a time to hate; A time of war, And a time of peace."* (Ecclesiastes 3:1-8)

Then Jonah prayed to the LORD his God from the fish's belly. And he said: "I cried out to the LORD because of my affliction, and He answered me. "Out of the belly of Sheol I cried, and You heard my voice." (Jonah 2:1, 2, 10)

"Therefore I will look to the LORD; I will wait for the God of my salvation; My God will hear me." (Micah 7:7)

According to the prophet of Ecclesiastes, there is a cycle for everything, including sickness and healing. As Pastor Ed Dobson once said, "If you are healthy, praise God. But if you are sick, just wait as you will probably get better."

That quote really isn't very comforting when you are sick or going through any other unpleasantness. However, if you will pray, use the power of the name of Jesus and throw out the Devil if he is at fault, the cycle in which you find yourself can be shortened.

God is full of mercy and grace. Jonah was thrown overboard for running from Nineveh and the will of God. Still, God gave him another chance. Jonah grudgingly obeyed His Heavenly Father, but he was not happy with the results of his obedience. God had to deal with that sour attitude. Jonah knew he was at fault and humbly asked God for His forgiveness. Of course, Father God did.

If your sickness is the result of your attitude or sin, confess it, ask God to forgive you, and accept His healing mercies. Remember, God will hear you if you pray like you mean it. Then God will hear you— no matter where you are.

– father Boyd

15

God Promises a Redeemer Who Will Bless All Mankind. Healing Is in the Redemption, and the Redeemer Has Come.

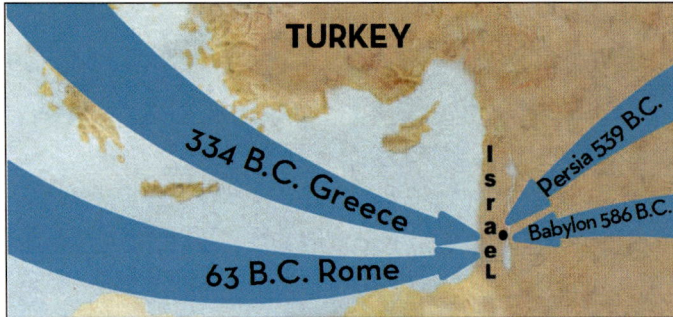

All roads of all ages led to the promised redemption.

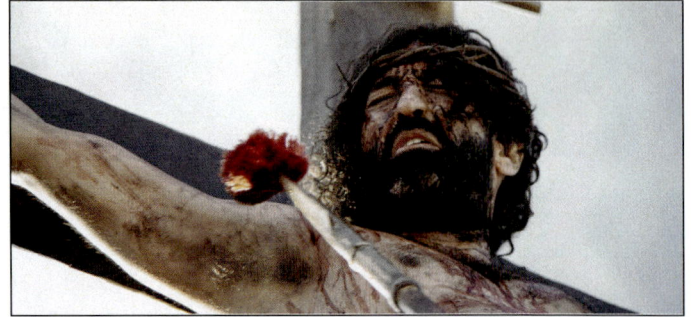

Jesus was offered a vinegar-saturated sponge to quench His thirst.

"I am poured out like water, and all My bones are out of joint; My heart is like wax; It has melted within Me. My strength is dried up like a potsherd, and My tongue clings to My jaws; You have brought Me to the dust of death. For dogs have surrounded Me; The congregation of the wicked has enclosed Me. They pierced My hands and My feet; I can count all My bones. They look and stare at Me. They divide My garments among them, and for My clothing they cast lots." (Psalm 22:14-18)

"I, the LORD, have called You in righteousness, and will hold Your hand; I will keep You and give You as a covenant to the people, As a light to the Gentiles, To open blind eyes, To bring out prisoners from the prison, [and] those who sit in darkness from the prison house." (Isaiah 42:6, 7)

One thousand years before the coming of the Redeemer, King David prophesied that when the Redeemer came, things would begin to happen. There would be absolutely no doubt that the One who came was who He said He was.

The way in which He was crucified was so horrendous that His bones were dislocated. The soldiers pierced His hands and His feet. As His bones came out of joint, it was almost as if they could have been counted. When He became so thirsty that He requested water, He was given a sponge dipped in vinegar. All around Him wicked people had gathered like dogs, staring at Jesus.

Those who loved Him were in the background and were not even allowed to come close to the suffering Savior. When the spear was thrust into His side while He was on the Cross, water came out. Then the soldiers divided His outer cloak and cast lots for the rest of His clothing.

Jesus suffered this cruel torture while His Father God allowed this punishment to happen to HIS ONLY BEGOTTEN SON. Why did God allow Jesus to suffer?

Quite simply, so that you and I could have our sins removed from God's eyes and live with Him in Heaven for all eternity. He also promised that Jesus would make an open, well-lit path to Heaven for the Gentiles. But God did not stop there. He also took all of the Christians who had died prior to His death on the Cross and those who were held in the prison houses.

If Father God, through His Son, Jesus Christ, was willing to do all of that so you would and I would have the option of living with Him and His Son in Heaven for all of eternity, can we not humble ourselves to accept this free gift?

– father Boyd

16

Jesus, the Messiah, Our Redeemer Is Born...
Prophecies Were Fulfilled.

An angel announced the good news to Mary.

Joseph was told not to put Mary away.

Christ was made flesh.

Now the birth of Jesus Christ was as follows: After His mother Mary was betrothed to Joseph, before they came together, she was found with child of the Holy Spirit. Then Joseph her husband, being a just man, and not wanting to make her a public example, was minded to put her away secretly. But while he thought about these things, behold, an angel of the Lord appeared to him in a dream, saying, "Joseph, son of David, do not be afraid to take to you Mary your wife, for that which is conceived in her is of the Holy Spirit. And she will bring forth a Son, and you shall call His name Jesus, for He will save His people from their sins." So all this was done that it might be fulfilled which was spoken by the Lord through the prophet, saying: "Behold, the virgin shall be with child, and bear a Son, and they shall call His name Immanuel," which is translated, "God with us." (Matthew 1:18-23)

"But you, Bethlehem, in the land of Judah, are not the least among the rulers of Judah; For out of you shall come a Ruler Who will shepherd My people Israel." (Matthew 2:6)

Matthew provides the reader with more details that reveal exactly how fantastic our God is! It blows my mind, as it should also blow yours, that when you read this passage from Matthew and take a step back, you simply have to ask, "How can this be?"

Picture this young girl probably in her early teens who is told that she is going to have a baby—when she has never been with a man. And she believed the messenger!

Joseph either loved Mary very much or he felt sorry for her. In Bible days when a Jewish girl was found with child out of wedlock, the Jews were supposed to stone her to death.

But just as Mary believed what the angel had told her, so did Joseph. The angel even went so far as to tell Joseph what he was to name the child. The angel quoted an Old Testament prophecy from Isaiah 7:14, which says, *"Therefore the LORD Himself will give you a sign: Behold, the virgin shall conceive and bear a Son, and shall call His name Immanuel."*

Matthew wrote that the name *Immanuel* means "God with us." Isn't that exactly what God has done for us since the day He was born?

Matthew also says that Jesus will also be a shepherd to us, taking care of us and providing what we need in this life—even to the point of not only saving us from our sins, but providing health and healing.

Is it any wonder why we should eagerly make Him our Lord and put Him in charge of our lives?

– father Boyd

Jesus Announces His Ministry in the Synagogue.

It did not matter what a person's problem was. Jesus would heal that person.

*"And Jesus went about all Galilee, teaching in their synagogues, preaching the gospel of the kingdom, and **healing all kinds of sickness and all kinds of disease among the people**. Then His fame went throughout all Syria; and **they brought to Him** all sick people who were afflicted with various diseases and **torments**, and those who were **demon-possessed**, epileptics, and paralytics; **and He healed them**.* (Matthew 4:23, 24)

"Ask, and it will be given to you; seek, and you will find; knock, and it will be opened to you. For everyone who asks receives, and he who seeks finds, and to him who knocks it will be opened." (Matthew 7:7, 8)

When evening had come, they brought to Him many who were demon-possessed. And He cast out the spirits with a word, and healed all who were sick, that it might be fulfilled which was spoken by Isaiah the prophet, saying: "He Himself took our infirmities and bore our sicknesses." (Matthew 8:16, 17)

Jesus officially announced His ministry in the Jewish synagogue by reading a prophetic passage from the Old Testament book of Isaiah, telling exactly the kind of Gospel He was going to preach and teach.

Far too often in today's world, we understand preaching to mean the use of words. And while that concept is indeed true, Jesus made it very clear that He came to preach the Gospel with actions, as well as with words.

With His words, Jesus made it very clear how a person can have eternal life (the story of redemption); and by His actions, He made it very clear that He also came to restore healing (His healing redemption).

Unless Jesus had an ulterior motive when He healed, He made it very clear that He healed ALL who came to Him for healing. It did not matter what their problem was; He healed them. In Matthew 7, Jesus said it as plainly as possible: (You) ask, and it will be given to you; if you seek healing, you will find it; if you knock, He will open the door for you. **But you may have to ask more than once; you may have to seek a while longer, and you may have to knock until He opens the door for you. But all He has promised, He will provide.**

How good and merciful is Father God; He tells us in writing what He intended to do hundreds of years before He did it. Then He did it so that numerous people could see what He had promised came true. Then He had these results written for all of us who followed Him to hear, to believe, and to trust Him to do the same for us.

There is no other god who has promised so much, will do so much, or ever will do what our God has done. *Are you willing to put your trust in Him?*

– father Boyd

God Heals Directly. God Heals Through Your Faith. God Heals Through Others.

She was healed when she touched His hem! He picked up his bed and walked! The leper was made clean!

But that you may know that the Son of Man has power on earth to forgive sins—then He said to the paralytic, "Arise, take up your bed, and go to your house." (Matthew 9:6)

*Then Jesus went about all the cities and villages, teaching in their synagogues, **preaching the gospel of the kingdom, and healing every sickness and every disease among the people.*** (Matthew 9:35)

*And Jesus said to him, "I will come and heal him."…Then Jesus said to the centurion, "Go your way; and **as you have believed,** so let it be done for you." And his servant was healed that same hour.* (Matthew 8:7, 13)

For she said to herself, "If only I may touch His garment, I shall be made well." But Jesus turned around, and when He saw her He said, "Be of good cheer, daughter; your faith has made you well." And the woman was made well from that hour. (Matthew 9:21-22)

And behold, a leper came and worshiped Him, saying, "Lord, if You are willing, You can make me clean." Then Jesus put out His hand and touched him, saying, "I am willing; be cleansed." Immediately his leprosy was cleansed. (Matthew 8:2, 3)

"Now when Jesus had come into Peter's house, He saw his wife's mother lying sick with a fever. So He touched her hand, and the fever left her. And she arose and served them." (Matthew 8:14, 15)

This study on *God's Healing Redemption* continues with reading of the healing miracles from Jesus directly, healing directly attributed to a person's faith, and healing through the faith of others. The first verse on this page shows Jesus not only healing, but forgiving the sins of the man He healed. Both the redemption from sins and the healing redemption of God are evidenced in this verse.

Then Jesus moved throughout the surrounding area, preaching through the use of words and visualizing His preaching by healing the sick. Sometimes Jesus chose to heal Himself; sometimes He healed because of the person's faith, and sometimes He healed because of others' asking.

Jesus' healing of the leper is significant for reasons that go beyond His healing of the leper. The stigma of lepers in that day was such that they were ignored and basically cast out of society. Never were they touched; so the leper was not sure that Jesus would even be willing to touch him.

But Jesus was not only willing to heal him; Jesus went beyond healing by touching this leper when He did so.

There is no place, nor is there anything you or I can do that will repulse Jesus or keep Him from comforting us.

– father Boyd

Jesus listened to the demon-possessed man.

God healed the demon-possessed man.

God sent the demons into the swine.

When evening had come, they brought to Him many who were demon-possessed. And He cast out the spirits with a word, and healed all who were sick, that it might be fulfilled which was spoken by Isaiah the prophet, saying: "He Himself took our infirmities and bore our sicknesses." (Matthew 8:16, 17)

When He had come to the other side…there met Him two demon-possessed men, coming out of the tombs, exceedingly fierce, so that no one could pass that way. And suddenly they cried out, saying, "What have we to do with You, Jesus, You Son of God? Have You come here to torment us before the time?" Now a good way off from them there was a herd of many swine feeding. So the demons begged Him, saying, "If You cast us out, permit us to go away into the herd of swine." And He said to them, "Go." So when they had come out, they went into the herd of swine. And suddenly the whole herd of swine ran violently down the steep place into the sea, and perished in the water. (Matthew 9:28-32)

"As they went out, behold, they brought to Him a man, mute and demon-possessed. And when the demon was cast out, the mute spoke…." (Matthew 9:32, 33)

"Lord, have mercy on my son, for he is an epileptic and suffers severely; for he often falls into the fire and often into the water."…And Jesus rebuked the demon, and it came out of him; and the child was cured from that very hour. (Matthew 17:15, 18)

…A woman of Canaan came from that region and cried out to Him, saying, "Have mercy on me, O Lord, Son of David! My daughter is severely demon-possessed."…Then Jesus answered and said to her, "O woman, great is your faith! Let it be to you as you desire." And her daughter was healed from that very hour. (Matthew 15:22, 28)

Verses in the Holy Bible that reference the work of the Devil in sickness, disease, ruined relationships, etc., are quite controversial.

Keep in mind that especially in developed countries at the time of Jesus, what was often referred to as *demon possession* then, now has numerous medical names applied to these seeming health-related problems.

So the first issue to address is what place the enemies of Jesus have. Those who follow Jesus must ask this question: "Is the Devil alive and active today?"

If you have tried other Jesus-taught ways or means of healing or if medicine doesn't work or only puts a bandaid on the problem, then the cause may very well be demon-related.

When the problem was demon-related, Jesus did only one thing; He ordered the demons to get out—to leave the stricken person.

Because He has, by "power of attorney," given us His power over the Enemy, that is also how we need to deal with this enemy of God.

– father Boyd

Additional Verses
Found in the Book of Matthew

"And great multitudes followed Him, and He healed them there." (Matthew 19:2)

Jesus healed every person who sought His help.

"And when Jesus went out He saw a great multitude; and He was moved with compassion for them, and healed their sick." (Matthew 14:14)

"Then great multitudes came to Him, having with them the lame, blind, mute, maimed, and many others; and they laid them down at Jesus' feet, and He healed them. So the multitude marveled when they saw the mute speaking, the maimed made whole, the lame walking, and the blind seeing; and they glorified the God of Israel."

(Matthew 15:30, 31)

*And behold, two blind men sitting by the road, when they heard that Jesus was passing by, cried out, saying, "Have mercy on us, O Lord, Son of David!" Then the multitude warned them that they should be quiet; but they cried out all the more, saying, "Have mercy on us, O Lord, Son of David!" So Jesus stood still and called them, and said, "**What do you want Me to do for you?**" They said to Him, "Lord, that our eyes may be opened." So Jesus had compassion and touched their eyes. And immediately their eyes received sight, and they followed Him.*

(Matthew 20:30-34)

"Then one was brought to Him who was demon-possessed, blind and mute; and He healed him, so that the blind and mute man both spoke and saw." (Matthew 12:22)

We now come to the end of the book of Matthew with only a few additional verses. This page will start and end with Jesus' showing exactly how far-reaching His compassion for people is.

Great multitudes came, and Jesus healed all of them who came of all their sicknesses—no matter what the problem was.

Once again we see that when the blind men came to Jesus, they came and would not be quiet or go away. They persisted until Jesus asked them what they wanted. When they told Jesus what they desired, Jesus healed them, showing then that if we want Jesus to heal us, we need to believe that He can and then keep believing until He does so.

It did not matter to Jesus if the people came in a multitude for healing or if there was only one, He healed all who came.

Yes, Jesus was the Son of David, and yes, Jesus is the Lord, and yes, Jesus proved that not only is He capable of healing, but His mercy is so great that He will heal you.

– father Boyd

Jesus Heals by Casting Out the Devil, and He Does It With Authority.

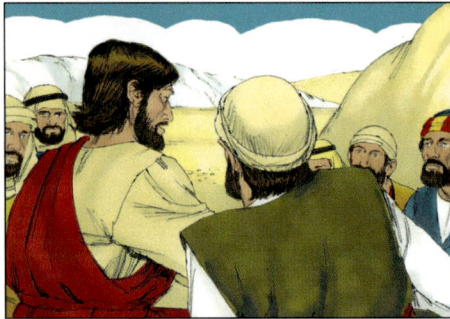

Jesus rebuked the demonic spirit.

Jesus taught with authority.

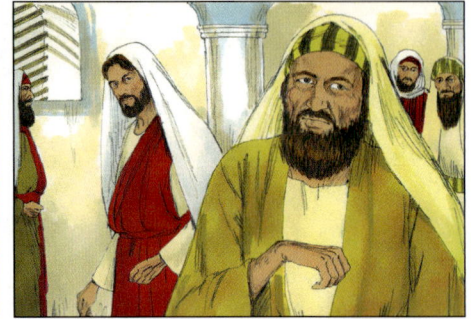

The man's withered hand was healed.

Then they went into Capernaum, and immediately on the Sabbath He entered the synagogue and taught. And they were astonished at His teaching, for He taught them as one having authority, and not as the scribes. Now there was a man in their synagogue with an unclean spirit. And he cried out, saying, "Let us alone! What have we to do with You, Jesus of Nazareth? Did You come to destroy us? I know who You are—the Holy One of God!" But Jesus rebuked him, saying, "Be quiet, and come out of him!" And when the unclean spirit had convulsed him and cried out with a loud voice, he came out of him. Then they were all amazed, so that they questioned among themselves, saying, "What is this? What new doctrine is this? For with authority He commands even the unclean spirits, and they obey Him." (Mark 1:21-27)

"Then He healed many who were sick with various diseases, and cast out many demons; and He did not allow the demons to speak, because they knew Him." (Mark 1:34)

But Jesus rebuked him, saying, "Be quiet, and come out of him!" And when the unclean spirit had convulsed him and cried out with a loud voice, he came out of him. (Mark 1:25-26)

And He [Jesus] entered the synagogue again, and a man was there who had a withered hand....And He said to the man who had the withered hand, "Step forward...Stretch out your hand." And he stretched it out, and his hand was restored as whole as the other. (Mark 3:1-5)

The writer of Mark was not one of the original apostles. He was probably the Mark who traveled with Paul, so he saw matters from a different perspective than the more compassionate Matthew.

It is interesting to note that Mark is much more in tune to the working of the Devil in the lives of people. I think it may be that, in the countries considered more progressive than others, the Devil has gone underground. Here in the United States, those with medical degrees and knowledge have given complicated names to the problems that were considered to be demon-related in the days of Jesus.

It is (and has been) the experience of many who have (and are involved) with the healing ministry, that Satan is alive and well.

When a sickness, disease, relationship, addiction, attitude, or mental situation occurs that cannot be addressed with the conventional healing methods, then we should consider that the problem may be demonic in nature. These situations must be addressed in the same manner in which Jesus addressed them. Take authority and order them to get out!

Jesus gave His children His authority over the Devil to use in casting them out.

– father Boyd

20a

The Authority of Jesus Extends Over the Devil and His Minions.

Jesus possessed the power to cast out demons and heal sicknesses.

And he cried out with a loud voice and said, "What have I to do with You, Jesus, Son of the Most High God? I implore You by God that You do not torment me." For He said to him, "Come out of the man, unclean spirit!" Then He asked him, "What is your name?" And he answered, saying, "My name is Legion; for we are many."… So all the demons begged Him, saying, "Send us to the swine, that we may enter them." And at once Jesus gave them permission…. (Mark 5:7-9, 12, 13)

…and she kept asking Him [Jesus] to cast the demon out of her daughter. But Jesus said to her, "Let the children be filled first, for it is not good to take the children's bread and throw it to the little dogs." And she answered and said to Him, "Yes, Lord, yet even the little dogs under the table eat from the children's crumbs." Then He said to her, "For this saying go your way; the demon has gone out of your daughter." And when she had come to her house, she found the demon gone out, and her daughter lying on the bed. (Mark 7:25-30)

So He asked his father, "How long has this been happening to him?" And he said, "From childhood. And often he [the demon] has thrown him both into the fire and into the water to destroy him. But if You can do anything, have compassion on us and help us." Jesus said to him, "If you can believe, all things are possible to him who believes." Immediately the father of the child cried out and said with tears, "Lord, I believe; help my unbelief!" When Jesus saw that the people came running together, He rebuked the unclean spirit, saying to it: "Deaf and dumb spirit, I command you, come out of him and enter him no more!" Then the spirit cried out, convulsed him greatly, and came out of him…. (Mark 9:21-26)

*"Then He [Jesus] appointed twelve, that they might be with Him and that He might send them out to preach, **and to have power to heal sicknesses and to cast out demons**."* (Mark 3:14, 15)

The book of Mark continues with more examples of the ministry of Jesus' dealing with the satanic. Clearly, numerous demons can be involved in the work of the Devil, as can be seen when they ALL begged Jesus to send them into the herd of pigs.

It should be noted that in each of these demonic occurences that Jesus never did anything other than take authority and command the demons—no matter how many there were—to get out.

The father realized that perhaps his faith still had some doubt in it, but he was sharp enough to ask for the help of Jesus for his shortcomings.

The mother with the daughter who had a demonic problem apparently was not Jewish. Still, she had faith in what Jesus could do, and she wanted for her daughter what Jesus could do.

Parents have the position, as the head of the family, to ask of Father God and Jesus for their family's needs, and God will hear.

When Jesus sent out the twelve disciples, notice what they were to do in addition to preaching that the kingdom of Heaven had arrived.

– father Boyd

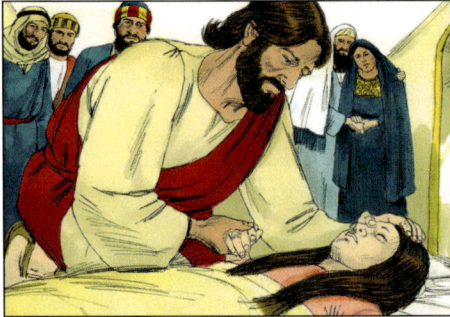
Jesus healed Jairus' daughter.

Jesus healed the man carried by four men.

Jesus healed Peter's mother-in-law.

"But Simon's wife's mother lay sick with a fever, and they told Him about her at once." (Mark 1:30)

Then they came to Him, bringing a paralytic who was carried by four men. And when they could not come near Him because of the crowd, they uncovered the roof where He was. So when they had broken through, they let down the bed on which the paralytic was lying. When Jesus saw their faith, He said to the paralytic, "Son, your sins are forgiven you."…"I say to you, arise, take up your bed, and go to your house." (Mark 2:3-5, 11)

Now a certain woman had a flow of blood for twelve years, and had suffered many things from many physicians. She had spent all that she had and was no better, but rather grew worse. When she heard about Jesus, she came behind Him in the crowd and touched His garment. For she said, "If only I may touch His clothes, I shall be made well." Immediately the fountain of her blood was dried up, and she felt in her body that she was healed of the affliction.…And He said to her, "Daughter, your faith has made you well. Go in peace, and be healed of your affliction." (Mark 5:25-29, 34)

"…Your daughter is dead. Why trouble the Teacher any further?" As soon as Jesus heard the word that was spoken, He said to the ruler of the synagogue, "Do not be afraid; only believe."…Then He took the child by the hand, and said to her, "Talitha, cumi," which is translated, "Little girl, I say to you, arise." Immediately the girl arose and walked… (Mark 5:35, 36, 41, 42)

Then they brought to Him one who was deaf and had an impediment in his speech, and they begged Him to put His hand on him.…Then, looking up to heaven, He sighed, and said to him, "Ephphatha," that is, "Be opened." Immediately his ears were opened, and the impediment of his tongue was loosed, and he spoke plainly. (Mark 7:32-35)

Simon Peter's mother-in-law only had a fever, but her suffering was enough to trigger a healing by Jesus. The Son of God is concerned with even the little things, which we might be hesitant to bring to Him.

The passage in Mark 2 is of special interest in that the paralytic's friends brought him to Jesus to be healed. In this case, Jesus responded to the faith of those who had brought their friend, believing Jesus could heal him.

Interestingly, Jesus first addressed the spiritual problem of the paralytic man and then healed him.

Sometimes your faith will move Jesus to heal you; sometimes it is a parent's faith; sometimes it is the faith of friends that moves Jesus to act. But it does seem that when the need was presented to Him, He always acted.

– father Boyd

Jesus heard the cry of those needing healing.

So He took the blind man by the hand and led him out of the town. And when He had spit on his eyes and put His hands on him, He asked him if he saw anything. And he looked up and said, "I see men like trees, walking." Then He put His hands on his eyes again and made him look up. And he was restored and saw everyone clearly. (Mark 8:23-25)

So Jesus answered and said to him [Bartimaeus], *"What do you want Me to do for you?" The blind man said to Him, "Rabboni, that I may receive my sight." Then Jesus said to him, "Go your way; your faith has made you well." And immediately he received his sight and followed Jesus on the road.* (Mark 10:51, 52)

"Therefore I say to you, whatever things you ask when you pray, believe that you receive them, and you will have them." (Mark 11:24)

Jesus answered and said to them, "Are you not therefore mistaken, because you do not know the Scriptures nor the power of God?" (Mark 12:24)

Why Jesus led the blind man out of town is anyone's guess. Why it took Jesus two times of placing His hands on the eyes of the blind man is also anyone's guess.

What is important to see is that if your healing is not perfectly completed the first time, you do not have to settle for a partial healing.

It is interesting to note that blind Bartimaeus came to Jesus, and Jesus had the audacity to ask the blind man what he wanted Jesus to do for him! After all, could not Jesus see what the problem was? We may never know until we get to Heaven why Jesus asked the question of Bartimaeus.

I personally believe this Scripture is teaching that when we come to Jesus asking, we should be specific as to what we are requesting. Then when you have asked specifically, believe what you have asked Him for.

Jesus also gave us a warning. We need to know what the Scriptures say in order to believe for the power of God to move in our lives.

Mark has recorded a number of healings that Jesus performed. He wants to do the same in your life, but you must believe that He is who He says He is and that He will do what He says He will do.

– father Boyd

Before Jesus ascended into Heaven, He commanded every believer to "Go, win, baptize, and teach."

And He said to them, "Go into all the world and preach the gospel to every creature. He who believes and is baptized will be saved; **but he who does not believe will be condemned. And these signs will follow those who believe**: *In My name they will cast out demons; they will speak with new tongues; they will take up serpents; and if they drink anything deadly, it will by no means hurt them; they will lay hands on the sick, and they will recover."*

(Mark 16:15-18)

"So then, after the Lord had spoken to them, He was received up into heaven, and sat down at the right hand of God. And they went out and preached everywhere, **the Lord working with them and confirming the word through the accompanying signs.** *Amen."* (Mark 16:19, 20)

The last great commandment that Jesus gave in both Matthew and in Mark are quite similar. I have chosen the one in Mark because it contains more specific details of what that last command of Jesus entailed.

Jesus made it very clear that while He expected His followers to preach His Gospel that the kingdom had come, He expected those who heard this preaching and teaching to believe and then to be baptized. However, He did not stop there.

Jesus told His disciples, and by inference, all of His followers since then what He expects of each of us.

Isn't it strange that, by and large, the organized church has chosen to ignore much of the Great Commission? Will we continue to ignore the part of the last commandment that Jesus gave to us or is it time to start to move back in that direction?

– father Boyd

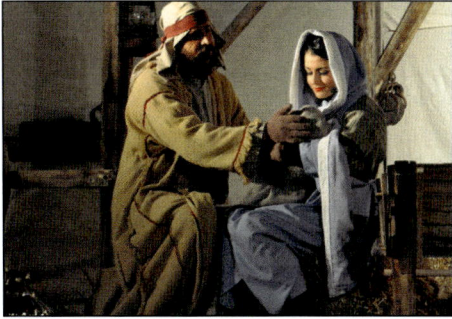

There was no room in the inn.

Jesus proclaimed liberty to the captives.

Jesus taught those who came to listen.

"So it was, that while they were there, the days were completed for her to be delivered. And she brought forth her firstborn Son, and wrapped Him in swaddling cloths, and laid Him in a manger, because there was no room for them in the inn." (Luke 2:6, 7)

"The Spirit of the LORD is upon Me, Because He has anointed Me to preach the gospel to the poor; He has sent Me to heal the brokenhearted, to proclaim liberty to the captives and recovery of sight to the blind, to set at liberty those who are oppressed; to proclaim the acceptable year of the LORD." (Luke 4:18, 19)

Now He arose from the synagogue and entered Simon's house. But Simon's wife's mother was sick with a high fever, and they made request of Him concerning her. So He stood over her and rebuked the fever, and it left her. And immediately she arose and served them. (Luke 4:38, 39)

"Now it happened on a certain day, as He was teaching, that there were Pharisees and teachers of the law sitting by, who had come out of every town of Galilee, Judea, and Jerusalem. And the power of the Lord was present to heal them." (Luke 5:17)

While going through the book of Luke and reviewing Jesus' healings, we need to keep in mind that Luke is recording what happened from the perspective of a doctor.

Luke starts out the message of Jesus by sharing some details of his birth. Can you imagine for a moment how the Creator came from the unspeakable splendor of Heaven to this sinful world and was then relegated to being born in a smelly, cold, and dirty barnyard?

In addition to there not being any room in any inn for Him, it later turned out that He did not find room in very many hearts either. I trust that is not the case in your heart and that you have made room for Him.

Jesus never accepted personal credit for preaching, healing, or deliverance. It was also the Holy Spirit's working within Jesus that caused the results. That fact has always been present from those days until now and will continue until Jesus returns. The power of the Holy Spirit is available to each of us to do what Jesus did. However, we must be willing to step out in faith and to put it to work for the kingdom.

According to the text found in Luke 4:18 and 19, Jesus equates broken-heartedness (or relational problems) in the same context as physical problems. Let Him deal with and heal those areas of problems in your life as well as the more obvious ones. Just a little side note: it appears that the fever that was afflicting Peter's mother-in-law was demonic because Jesus rebuked it, and it left.

– father Boyd

When It Comes to Healing, Jesus Is Always Willing.

Jesus did not fear the contagion of a leprous man.

Jesus healed the multitudes of their diseases.

And it happened when He was in a certain city, that behold, a man who was full of leprosy saw Jesus; and he fell on his face and implored Him, saying, "Lord, if You are willing, You can make me clean." Then He put out His hand and touched him, saying, "I am willing; be cleansed." Immediately the leprosy left him. (Luke 5:12, 13)

And when He had looked around at them all, He said to the man, "Stretch out your hand." And he did so, and his hand was restored as whole as the other. (Luke 6:10)

*"And He came down with them and stood on a level place with a crowd of His disciples and a great multitude of people from all Judea and Jerusalem, and from the seacoast of Tyre and Sidon, who came to hear Him and be healed of their diseases, as well as those who were tormented with unclean spirits. **And they were healed**."* (Luke 6:17, 18)

"So I say to you, ask, and it will be given to you; seek, and you will find; knock, and it will be opened to you. For everyone who asks receives, and he who seeks finds, and to him who knocks it will be opened." (Luke 11:9, 10)

"A disciple is not above his teacher, but everyone who is perfectly trained will be like his teacher." (Luke 6:40)

The fortieth verse of the sixth chapter is very important to us today—especially if we consider ourselves to be disciples of Christ.

The man who begged Jesus to heal him of his leprosy was not infected with only a little bit of the disease. He was leprous from head to toe. I would imagine he not only looked gross, but no doubt, he also smelled badly. He was probably so grotesque-looking from the debilitating effects of the disease that he could not imagine Jesus even being willing to heal him.

But what did Jesus say? "I am willing."

Jesus is not a respecter of persons, and if He was willing to heal a person who looked bad, smelled bad, and had no hope of ever being normal again or enjoying a normal life again, don't you think He can and will heal you also?

Jesus healed all who came seeking. And if you will ask and seek and knock, He will open. If you are willing to seek Him, you will find Him.

As always, it is YOUR choice.

– father Boyd

Jesus Again Deals With the Demonic Beings That Are Affecting the People.

Jesus healed the woman who could not stand straight.

Jesus healed the man with the spirit of the unclean demon.

Now in the synagogue there was a man who had a spirit of an unclean demon. And he cried out with a loud voice, saying, "Let us alone! What have we to do with You, Jesus of Nazareth? Did You come to destroy us? I know who You are—the Holy One of God!" But Jesus rebuked him, saying, "Be quiet, and come out of him!" And when the demon had thrown him in their midst, it came out of him and did not hurt him. (Luke 4:33-35)

When the sun was setting, all those who had any that were sick with various diseases brought them to Him; and He laid His hands on every one of them and healed them. And demons also came out of many, crying out and saying, "You are the Christ, the Son of God!" And He, rebuking them, did not allow them to speak, for they knew that He was the Christ. (Luke 4:40, 41)

*Now He was teaching in one of the synagogues on the Sabbath. And behold, there was a woman who had **a spirit of infirmity** eighteen years, and was bent over and could in no way raise herself up. But when Jesus saw her, He called her to Him and said to her, "Woman, you are loosed from your infirmity." And He laid His hands on her, and immediately she was made straight, and glorified God.* (Luke 13:10-13)

*Suddenly a man…cried out, saying, "Teacher, I implore You, look on my son, for he is my only child. And behold, a spirit seizes him, and he suddenly cries out; it convulses him so that he foams at the mouth; and it departs from him with great difficulty, bruising him. So I implored Your disciples to cast it out, but they could not." Then Jesus answered and said, "O faithless and perverse generation, how long shall I be with you and bear with you? Bring your son here." And as he was still coming, the demon threw him down and convulsed him. Then **Jesus rebuked the unclean spirit, healed the child, and gave him back to his father.*** (Luke 9:38-42)

I have been absolutely amazed as I have put these Scriptures together. Exactly how much of Jesus' time related to healing and how much time He needed to deal with the Devil is astounding. I find this especially amazing since this problem now seems to be swept under the rug. Apparently today's Christians would rather title similar problems with complicated, foreign-sounding names, seek counseling, take pills or injections, or embrace any other possible treatment except face the truth. Granted, these medical choices often help somewhat, but the bottom line is that the standard method of treatment is no more than "applying a bandaid."

I also find it interesting that the demonic world knew exactly who Jesus was; yet so often, mankind does not seem to have a clue. Jesus was concerned that He would soon be leaving and that perhaps His followers had not yet mastered the art of deliverance. Only then did the questions surface:

1. How does today's church understand the work of the Devil—especially in the area of healing?

2. Shouldn't the church take the commandment of Jesus seriously when He told us to cast out demons and then gave us all the authority to use His name to do so?

– father Boyd

24a Jesus Christ Is NO Respecter of Persons; He Loves All of Mankind.

The centurion sought help for his servant.

The men brought their friend to Jesus.

Jesus healed the paralyzed man.

*And a certain centurion's servant, who was dear to him, was sick and **ready to die**. So when he heard about Jesus, he sent elders of the Jews to Him, pleading with Him to come and heal his servant. And when they came to Jesus, they begged Him earnestly, saying that the one for whom He should do this was deserving…Then Jesus went with them. And when He was already not far from the house, the centurion sent friends to Him, saying to Him, "Lord, do not trouble Yourself, for I am not worthy that You should enter under my roof.…But say the word, and my servant will be healed."…When Jesus heard these things, He…said to the crowd that followed Him, "I say to you, **I have not found such great faith, not even in Israel!**" And those who were sent, returning to the house, found the servant well who had been sick.* (Luke 7:2-10)

*Then behold, men brought on a bed a man who was paralyzed…And when they could not find how they might bring him in, because of the crowd, they went up on the housetop and let him down with his bed through the tiling into the midst before Jesus. **When He saw their faith**, He said to him, "**Man, your sins are forgiven you.**"…I say to you, arise, take up your bed, and go to your house."* (Luke 5:18-20, 24)

*And when He came near the gate of the city, behold, a dead man was being carried out, the only son of his mother; and she was a widow.…When the Lord saw her, **He had compassion on her** and said to her, "Do not weep."…And He said, "Young man, I say to you, arise." So he who was dead sat up.…* (Luke 7:12-15)

*And behold, there was a certain man before Him who had dropsy [a swelling of the body causing excess fluids]. And Jesus, answering, spoke to the lawyers and Pharisees, saying, "Is it lawful to heal on the Sabbath?" But they kept silent. And **He took him and healed him**, and let him go.* (Luke 14:2-4)

Jesus really is no respecter of person. A Roman military man with a sick servant sent his friends (who were probably Jewish) to Jesus on behalf of that servant—either a hired man or a slave. What did Jesus do? He healed him without even seeing him! Trust in Jesus is all that seems to matter.

In the first passage mentioned, friends brought the request to Jesus. In the second passage, friends actually brought their paralyzed friend to the Savior. In response to their faith and trust in the fact that He would heal, Jesus healed their friend.

Jesus also heals out of compassion. In Luke 7, He raised a dead son and returned him to his mother. And finally, Jesus uses healing when he wants to make a point.

As I have already stated, Jesus is NO respecter of persons.

– father Boyd

25   Jesus Sent Out His Disciples to Do What He Did; As He Sent Them, So He Also Sends Us.

One leper returned to thank Jesus for healing him.

Jesus gave His disciples power to heal.

And they [the ten lepers] *lifted up their voices and said, "Jesus, Master, have mercy on us!" So when He saw them, He said to them,* **"Go, show yourselves to the priests."** *And so it was that as they went, they were cleansed. And one of them, when he saw that he was healed, returned, and with a loud voice glorified God…And He said to him, "Arise, go your way.* **Your faith has made you well."** (Luke 17:13-15, 19)

Now a woman, having a flow of blood for twelve years, who had spent all her livelihood on physicians and could not be healed by any, came from behind and touched the border of His garment. And immediately her flow of blood stopped. And Jesus said, "Who touched Me?…Daughter, be of good cheer; **your faith has made you well. Go in peace."** (Luke 8:43-45, 48)

And one of them struck the servant of the high priest and cut off his right ear. But Jesus answered and said, "Permit even this." And **He touched his ear and healed him.** (Luke 22:50, 51)

"Then He called His twelve disciples together and gave them power and authority over all demons, and to cure diseases. **He sent them to preach the kingdom of God and to heal the sick."** (Luke 9:1, 2)

I find it interesting that the lepers were healed on the way to the temple where their healing would be certified. Nine of them continued to the temple, but one thought it more prudent to return to Jesus and thank Him for the healing miracle.

In this case as well as in the case of the woman who was healed, Jesus told both of them that their faith had made them well. Could Jesus have meant that not only had their faith been responsible for their physical healing, but also that the same faith that brought healing of the body also earned them salvation and eternal life. Could they have been made completely whole—body and soul?

The last miracle that Jesus personally performed on this earth was for a soldier who was present with others to take Jesus into custody. Jesus' imprisonment would eventually bring brutal treatment and finally crucifixion. Jesus never stopped His healing ministry, and He never showed any partiality when He healed.

The verses in Luke 9 have been placed at the end of this dialogue of the book of Luke because, even as Jesus sent out the twelve and gave them His power to preach, to heal, and to have power over all demons, even so, He gave us His power through the Holy Spirit to go and do likewise.

– father Boyd

26 | The Most Recognized Verse in the Bible: John 3:16

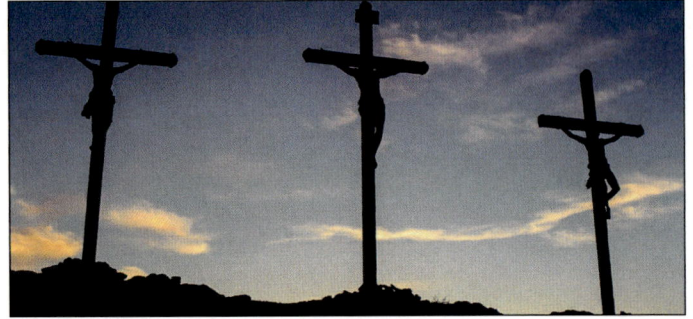

Jesus Christ suffered untold torture before He died on the Cross for all of mankind.

*"For God so loved the world that He gave His only begotten Son, that **whoever believes in Him should not perish but have everlasting life**. For God did not send His Son into the world to condemn the world, but that the world through Him might be saved."* (John 3:16, 17)

"Then a great multitude followed Him, because they saw His signs which He performed on those who were diseased." (John 6:2)

*…And there was a certain nobleman whose son was sick at Capernaum. When he heard that Jesus had come out of Judea into Galilee, he went to Him and implored Him to come down and heal his son, for he was at the point of death. Then Jesus said to him, "Unless you people see signs and wonders, you will by no means believe." The nobleman said to Him, "Sir, come down before my child dies!" Jesus said to him, "Go your way; your son lives." **So the man believed** the word that Jesus spoke to him, and he went his way. And as he was now going down, his servants met him and told him, saying, "Your son lives!"* (John 4:46-51)

God made this world, and Genesis records that He made it good. Originally, mankind spoiled perfection with disobedient sin, which only grew worse from that point. But God still loved what He had created so much that He enacted a plan so that all mankind could be redeemed.

Believing in Father God and His Son, Jesus Christ, is not something that mankind can explain by reason; rather, it must be taken by faith.

In his book *Amazing Truths*, Dr. John Guillen puts it this way: "Seek not to understand so that you may believe, but believe that you may understand, for unless you believe, you will not understand."

Unless a person is willing to believe that God exists, that He has done what He says He has done and that He sent His Son, Jesus Christ, not only to die and to redeem you from your sins, but also to redeem you from your sickness, you will not be redeemed.

Jesus has made it very clear that not only could He heal, He did, in fact, heal while He was among us. And He then made it clear that healing is still accomplished through faith in His name.

– father Boyd

Lazarus was raised from the dead.

Jesus mixed saliva and clay for healing.

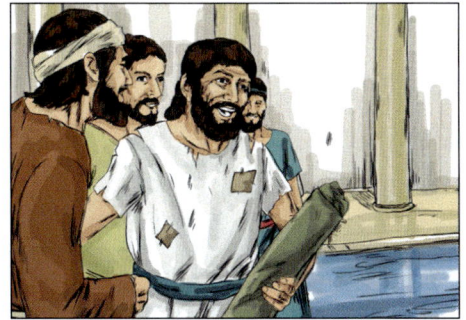
Jesus healed the infirm man.

Believe Me that I am in the Father and the Father in Me, or else believe Me for the sake of the works themselves. "Most assuredly, I say to you, he who believes in Me, the works [including healing] that I do he will do also; and greater works than these he will do, because I go to My Father. And whatever you ask in My name, that I will do, that the Father may be glorified in the Son. If you ask anything in My name, I will do it. (John 14:11-14)

Jesus said to her, "Did I not say to you that if you would believe you would see the glory of God?" Then…Jesus lifted up His eyes and said, "Father, I thank You that You have heard Me. And I know that You always hear Me, but because of the people who are standing by I said this, that they may believe that You sent Me." Now when He had said these things, He cried with a loud voice, "Lazarus, come forth!" And he who had died came out…. (John 11:40-43)

Now a certain man was there who had an infirmity thirty-eight years. When Jesus saw him lying there, and knew that he already had been in that condition a long time, He said to him, "Do you want to be made well?" [Then] Jesus said to him, "Rise, take up your bed and walk." And immediately the man was made well, took up his bed, and walked. (John 5:5-9)

Now as Jesus passed by, He saw a man who was blind from birth…When He had said these things, He spat on the ground and made clay with the saliva; and He anointed the eyes of the blind man with the clay. And He said to him, "Go, wash in the pool of Siloam"…So he went and washed, and came back seeing. (John 9:1-7)

Jesus said that one of the reasons why we should believe in both God and Himself is because of the works that He did. And those healing works that He did are still being done is His name today. As a result, the glory to and of the Father continues.

Jesus asked the man by the pool if he wanted to be healed. The man never answered the question. When you come to Jesus for healing, make sure you tell Him you want to be healed.

There is so much that could be said, but the Word of God, through the power of the Holy Spirit, is more than adequate.

Remember, the Holy Spirit will give you the faith to believe and the faith (or trust) to believe for your salvation and eternal life. This same faith and trust will provide your healing right now—while you are here on this earth.

- father Boyd

The Roman soldiers imprisoned the innocent Son of God.

Christ was wounded for mankind's transgressions.

"Surely He has borne our griefs
And carried our sorrows;
Yet we esteemed Him stricken,
Smitten by God, and afflicted.
But He was wounded for our transgressions,
He was bruised for our iniquities;
The chastisement for our peace was upon Him,
And by His stripes we are healed."

(Isaiah 53:4, 5)

Many prophesies throughout the Old Testament tell of the coming of Jesus Christ.

The prophecy found in Isaiah 53 makes it very clear that Jesus was coming to redeem us from our sins and that His atonement also included "complete" healing for our physical bodies.

The Hebrew words for *grief* and *sorrows* specifically means "physical afflictions." But just as the words of John 3:16 make it plain that the sacrifice was sufficient for our sins, Jesus must be received by us before we can have what He promised.

The same is true for a person's temporal physical healing. If you want healing, you must first ask for it.

Then just as with salvation from your sins, you must believe and trust that what Jesus did was for you.

– father Boyd

Jesus' authority and power was made available to His followers through the power of Holy Spirit.

"Then fear came upon every soul, and many wonders and signs were done through the apostles." (Acts 2:43)

"Now, Lord, look on their threats, and grant to Your servants that with all boldness they may speak Your word, by stretching out Your hand to heal, and that signs and wonders may be done through the name of Your holy Servant Jesus." (Acts 4:29, 30)

"Therefore they stayed there a long time, speaking boldly in the Lord, who was bearing witness to the word of His grace, granting signs and wonders to be done by their hands." (Acts 14:3)

"And it happened that the father of Publius lay sick of a fever and dysentery. Paul went in to him and prayed, and he laid his hands on him and healed him. So when this was done, the rest of those on the island who had diseases also came and were healed." (Acts 28:8-9)

"And Stephen, full of faith and power, did great wonders and signs among the people." (Acts 6:8)

"And through the hands of the apostles many signs and wonders were done among the people....so that they brought the sick out into the streets and laid them on beds and couches, that at least the shadow of Peter passing by might fall on some of them." (Acts 5:12, 15)

Jesus' coming to earth and healing people was not a "one-time" happening. When He walked this earth, He said He would send the Holy Spirit to us so that His disciples and all who followed thereafter would preach and teach as He did.

The power of Jesus to heal was so effective that when the sick were brought out to the street, they were healed if the shadow of Peter merely fell on them.

No one can act in all boldness and all that implies if he is operating under his own power. Only when a person is acting under the authority of the name of Jesus and in the power of the Holy Spirit can real wonders and signs follow.

When reading of Stephen and the wonders and signs that he did, the Bible makes it abundantly clear that what he accomplished was because he was full of faith and power.

Jesus had made it very clear that after He left this earth, His authority and power would always be available through the power of the Holy Spirit operating within people full of faith and power.

That same faith and power operates through people for the benefit of others. It will also operate in families for their children. It will also directly operate in individual lives. Jesus will meet your needs when you go to Him in faith and trust.

– father Boyd

27a   The Lord Knows Whom He Chooses for His Work.

Ananias laid hands on Saul to heal him.

He walked and leaped and praised God!

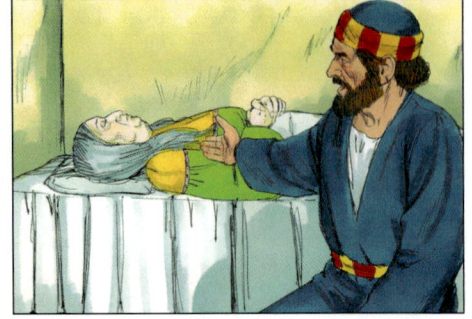

Peter was called to the side of Dorcas.

Now there was a certain disciple at Damascus named Ananias; and to him the Lord said in a vision…And Ananias… entered the house; and laying his hands on him he said, "Brother Saul, the Lord Jesus…has sent me that you may receive your sight and be filled with the Holy Spirit." Immediately there fell from his eyes something like scales…. (Acts 9:10, 17, 18)

And a certain man lame from his mother's womb was carried, whom they laid daily at the gate of the temple… who, seeing Peter and John about to go into the temple, asked for alms. And fixing his eyes on him, with John, Peter said, "Look at us…Silver and gold I do not have, but what I do have I give you: In the name of Jesus Christ of Nazareth, rise up and walk." And he took him by the right hand and lifted him up, and immediately his feet and ankle bones received strength. So he, leaping up, stood and walked and entered the temple with them—walking, leaping, and praising God. (Acts 3:2-8)

Now it came to pass, as Peter went through all parts of the country, that he also came down to the saints who dwelt in Lydda. There he found a certain man named Aeneas, who had been bedridden eight years and was paralyzed. And Peter said to him, "Aeneas, Jesus the Christ heals you. Arise and make your bed." Then he arose immediately. (Acts 9:32-34)

Now God worked unusual miracles by the hands of Paul, so that even handkerchiefs or aprons were brought from his body to the sick, and the diseases left them and the evil spirits went out of them. (Acts 19:11-12)

The ministry of Paul (formerly Saul of Tarsus) began sometime after Jesus had departed. Most readers of the Word of God know the story of his persecution of Christians and his subsequent conversion. At the time, Jesus spoke to Paul on the road; he was also struck with blindness and had to be led to Damascus.

While Saul was in Damascus, God reached out via a vision to an ordinary disciple who was needed for His work. God told Ananias that he had a healing job for him to perform. Ananias obeyed God, Paul's sight was restored, and the ministry that God had in mind for Paul began.

As Peter and John walked into the temple, probably using the same path and gate that Jesus had often used when He walked into the temple, they healed a man who only expected and hoped to receive some little monetary help for his very survival.

The healing power from God through the Holy Spirit was so strong that even handkerchiefs and Paul's tent-making apron was enough to bring healing to those who wanted it.

– father Boyd

The Disciples Did What Jesus Did.

Peter was used to heal Dorcas.

Paul healed a man who desired healing.

Paul healed the father of Publius and others.

*At Joppa there was a certain disciple named Tabitha, which is translated Dorcas. This woman was full of good works and charitable deeds which she did. But it happened in those days **that she became sick and died**. When they had washed her, they laid her in an upper room. And since Lydda was near Joppa, and the disciples had heard that Peter was there, they sent two men to him, imploring him not to delay in coming to them. Then Peter arose and went with them. When he had come, they brought him to the upper room. And all the widows stood by him weeping, showing the tunics and garments which Dorcas had made while she was with them. But **Peter put them all out, and knelt down and prayed**. And turning to the body he said, "Tabitha, arise." And **she opened her eyes, and when she saw Peter she sat up.** (Acts 9:36-40)*

*And in Lystra a certain man without strength in his feet was sitting, a cripple from his mother's womb, who had never walked. This man heard Paul speaking. Paul, observing him intently and **seeing that he had faith to be healed**, said with a loud voice, "Stand up straight on your feet!" And he leaped and walked. (Acts 14:8-10)*

*And it happened that the father of Publius lay sick of a fever and dysentery. Paul went in to him and prayed, and **he laid his hands on him and healed him**. So when this was done, the rest of those on the island who had diseases also came and were healed. (Acts 28:8, 9)*

*Then Philip went down to the city of Samaria and preached Christ to them. And the multitudes with one accord heeded the things spoken by Philip, **hearing and seeing the miracles which he did**. For unclean spirits, crying with a loud voice, came out of many who were possessed; and many who were paralyzed and lame were healed. (Acts 8:5-7)*

As we continue to follow the healings that took place after Jesus returned to Heaven, it is obvious that every type of healing that Jeus did while He was here was also done by His disciples and followers after He returned to His Father.

Peter sent everyone out of the room and prayed for direction. He prayed, he spoke, and Dorcas returned from the dead.

Then Paul was led by the Holy Spirit to see the faith of a lifelong cripple, and Paul spoke words of healing. Paul also prayed in faith for the father of Publius to be healed. Not only was Publius healed, so were the rest of the islanders who were sick and suffering with various diseases.

And finally, God is using a former deacon in the ministry of healing and dliverance.

I believe it is safe to say that, according to the book of Acts, the ministry of healing has been passed on from Jesus.

– father Boyd

28 Often Faith to Hear and Do As Father God Directs May Not Make Sense.

Abraham believed God.

His faith was accounted for righteousness.

God gives diversities of gifts.

For what does the Scripture say? "**Abraham believed God,** *and it was accounted to him for righteousness."…But to him who does not work but believes on Him who justifies the ungodly,* **his faith is accounted for righteousness.** (Romans 4:3, 5)

"in mighty signs and wonders, **by the power of the Spirit of God,** *so that from Jerusalem and round about to Illyricum I have fully preached the gospel of Christ."* (Romans 15:19)

*"Now t***o Him who is able to establish you** *according to my* [Paul speaking] *gospel and the preaching of Jesus Christ, according to the revelation of the mystery kept secret since the world began but now made manifest, and by the prophetic Scriptures made known to all nations, according to* **the commandment of the everlasting God, for obedience to the faith**—*to God, alone wise, be glory through Jesus Christ forever. Amen."* (Romans 16:25-27)

"There are diversities of gifts, but the same Spirit. There are differences of ministries, but the same Lord. And there are diversities of activities, but it is the same God who works all in all. But the manifestation of the Spirit is given to each one for the profit of all: for to one is given the word of wisdom through the Spirit, to another the word of knowledge through the same Spirit, to **another faith by the same Spirit, to another gifts of healings by the same Spirit,** *to another the working of miracles, to another prophecy,* **to another discerning of spirits,** *to another different kinds of tongues, to another the interpretation of tongues.* **But one and the same Spirit works all these things, distributing to each one individually as He wills.**" (I Corinthians 12:4-11)

The writer of Romans clearly presents that what matters most to Father God is how we each listen and obey His words and His leading. God counts this personal faith as righteousness.

When we follow the leading of the Word of God, mighty signs and wonders can work through us by the power of the Holy Spirit.

God Himself, through Jesus Christ, firmly sets us into His kingdom through faith, and He does this so that He might get all the glory.

This same Holy Spirit is He who provides the Christian with various gifts. Very few Christians will receive all of the gifts over their lifetime, but each of the gifts will be given as needed in each individual situation. Some of these gifts are very helpful for Christians in the area of healing, including faith, words of knowledge, words of wisdom, miracles, and discerning of spirits.

When the writer lists the gift of healings, the word "healings" is plural—not the word "gift." This plurality may be because so many different kinds of healing are needed in the life of the Christian. Each required healing can be different from others that were needed in times past. It is likely that many persons are needed to address all of the different needs—both in others and even in a Christian's personal life.

– father Boyd

29 Jesus Supplied the Spirit;
the Spirit Supplies the Power.

God sent the power of the Holy Spirit at Pentecost.

*"Therefore He who supplies the Spirit to you and works miracles among you, does He do it by the works of the law, or **by the hearing of faith?**"* (Galatians 3:5)

*"For our gospel did not come to you in word only, **but also in power, and in the Holy Spirit….**"* (I Thessalonians 1:5)

"For indeed he [Epaphroditus] *was sick almost unto death; but God had mercy on him…."* (Philippians 2:27)

*"Be anxious for nothing, but in everything by prayer and supplication, with thanksgiving, let your requests be made known to God; **and the peace of God, which surpasses all understanding,** will guard your hearts and minds through Christ Jesus."* (Philippians 4:6, 7)

Before Jesus departed this earth, He had told the disciples to wait, and He would send the Holy Spirit. They waited in the upper room, and Jesus did indeed send the Holy Spirit, and all of the "gifts of the Spirit" were in evidence from that time forward.

The writer of the Thessalonians again makes it clear that the Gospel is more than simply words. What accompanies the preaching of the Word should be miracles—available through the power of the Holy Spirit.

Sickness also comes to the Christian—sometimes even taking the follower of Jesus to the point of death. Only through God's mercy does that healing occur.

Paul, the author of Philippians, makes quite plain that the Christian should not be anxious for anything. Instead, every believer is to put his concerns into prayer and petitions to Father God. We should, along with our requests, take the opportunity to thank God for all He has already done, as well as to give thanks for what He is going to do.

Father God will provide a peace that is way beyond our understanding and will guard the attitude of our heart and mind because of what Jesus Christ has done.

Never forget that Father God is interested in YOUR physical, mental, and social well-being.

– father Boyd

30

God Will Bear Witness to Your Faith With Signs and Wonders.

The heroes of faith prayed for the power of God.

*"Now **faith is the substance of things hoped for**, the evidence of things not seen."* (Hebrews 11:1)

*"God also bearing witness both with signs and wonders, with various miracles, and gifts of the Holy Spirit, **according to His own will?**"* (Hebrews 2:4)

*"My brethren, **count it all joy when you fall into various trials**, knowing that the testing of your faith produces patience. But let patience have its perfect work, that you may be perfect and complete, lacking nothing. **If any of you lacks wisdom, let him ask of God**, who gives to all liberally and without reproach, and **it will be given to him. But let him ask in faith, with no doubting**, for he who doubts is like a wave of the sea driven and tossed by the wind."* (James 1:2-6)

"If any of you lacks wisdom, let him ask of God, who gives to all liberally and without reproach, and it will be given to him." (James 1:5)

*"...**you do not have because you do not ask.** You ask and do not receive, because you ask amiss, that you may spend it on your pleasures."* (James 4:2, 3)

*"Is anyone among you sick? Let him call for the elders of the church, and let them pray over him, anointing him with oil in the name of the Lord. **And the prayer of faith will save the sick**, and the Lord will raise him up. And if he has committed sins, he will be forgiven."* (James 5:14, 15)

Hebrews 11:1, one of the most quoted verses in the Bible, is also one of the most difficult verses to verbalize and explain. The obvious explanation is that if we ask for something that can be seen, our request cannot be considered faith. The Scripture is clear: if we ask for something from Father God that we cannot see but are willing to trust Him to provide it, that is showing faith.

When God provides, He often does so in ways that will be a sign. We will be amazed by what God will do, and what He does will be considered a miracle.

But then, James takes us to task in that we may have to wait while Father God checks to see if we will really trust Him to give us what we asked for.

James cautions us not to give in to doubt. Some of the heroes of the faith doubted and tried to "help" God when it would have been better if they had simply waited a while longer.

James continues on to say that often we do not have because we have never asked. Or if we did ask, we asked selfishly, or as he says, we asked "amiss."

When you call for the elders of the church and they pray over you and anoint you with oil, then the elders should do so in the faith that the Lord will indeed heal the sick person.

– father Boyd

By His stripes we are healed.

"who Himself bore our sins in His own body on the tree, that we, having died to sins, might live for righteousness— **by whose stripes you were healed."** *(I Peter 2:24)*

"Now this is the confidence that we have in Him, that **if we ask anything according to His will, He hears us.** *And if we know that* **He hears us, whatever we ask,** *we know that we have the petitions that we have asked of Him."* (I John 5:14, 15)

"Beloved, **I pray that you may prosper in all things** *and be in health,* **just as your soul prospers."** *(3 John 2)*

"He [Jesus] was in the world, and the world was made through Him, and [still] the world did not know Him. He came to His own, and His own did not receive Him. **But as many as received Him, to them He gave the right to become children of God, to those who believe in His name."** *(John 1:10-12)*

*"***For the time will come when they will not endure sound doctrine,** *but according to their own desires, because they have itching ears, they will heap up for themselves teachers; and they will turn their ears away from the truth, and be turned aside to fables. But you be watchful in all things* [**including your healing**]*, endure afflictions, do the work of an evangelist, fulfill your ministry. For I am already being poured out as a drink offering, and the time of my departure is at hand. I have fought the good fight, I have finished the race, I have kept the faith."* (II Timothy 4:3-7)

Peter is quoting Isaiah when he wrote under the inspiration of the Holy Spirit, *"...by whose stripes you were healed."* Peter had no doubt that the atonement which Jesus brought at Calvary covered redemption from our sins. The brutal suffering, especially the forty stripes that Jesus bore on His back, was more than sufficent to restore health and healing to mankind as well.

John takes it to the next step in that he equates our health to how we are prospering in the spiritual department. John cannot understand how a world that was brought into existence could fail to recognize and receive Him. He warns Christians to be watchful in all things, including their health and healing. In other words, don't become confused about the words that you read in the Bible regarding the fact that healing is yours. Be reminded that Jesus is capable and willing to provide healing.

Paul has spent many years in the ministry and suffered much, and he is about to die. As he said, he has worked hard and suffered much. In a short summary, Paul expected to die for preaching the Gospel. We too will die, but what will we die for?

- father Boyd

Jesus Is Coming Again—Maybe Today!
Are You Ready?

*And there shall be no more curse, but the throne of God and of the Lamb shall be in it, and His servants shall serve Him. They shall see His face, and His name shall be on their foreheads. There shall be no night there: They need no lamp nor light of the sun, for the Lord God gives them light. And they shall reign forever and ever. Then he said to me, "**These words are faithful and true.**" And the Lord God of the holy prophets sent His angel to show His servants the things which must shortly take place. "**Behold, I am coming quickly!** Blessed is he who keeps the words of the prophecy of this book."* (Revelation 22:3-7)

*And He said to them, "Go into all the world and preach the gospel to every creature. He who believes and is baptized will be saved; but he who does not believe will be condemned. And these signs will follow those who believe: In My name they will cast out demons; they will speak with new tongues; they will take up serpents; and if they drink anything deadly, it will by no means hurt them; **they will lay hands on the sick, and they will recover.**"*

(Mark 16:15-18)

You Must Believe by Faith For Your Healing, but You Will Encounter a Spiritual Battle.

Jesus paid the price for all of mankind to have an eternal home in Heaven.

"Finally, my brethren, be strong in the Lord and in the power of His might. Put on the whole armor of God, that you may be able to stand against the wiles of the devil. For we do not wrestle against flesh and blood, but against principalities, against powers, against the rulers of the darkness of this age, against spiritual hosts of wickedness in the heavenly places. Therefore take up the whole armor of God, that you may be able to withstand in the evil day, and having done all, to stand." (Ephesians 6:10-13)

"Therefore humble yourselves under the mighty hand of God, that He may exalt you in due time, casting all your care upon Him, for He cares for you. Be sober, be vigilant; because your adversary the devil walks about like a roaring lion, seeking whom he may devour. Resist him, steadfast in the faith, knowing that the same sufferings are experienced by your brotherhood in the world. But may the God of all grace, who called us to His eternal glory by Christ Jesus, after you have suffered a while, perfect, establish, strengthen, and settle you. To Him be the glory and the dominion forever and ever. Amen." (I Peter 5:6-11)

"You are of God, little children, and have overcome them, because He who is in you is greater than he who is in the world." (I John 4:4)

"And you, being dead in your trespasses and the uncircumcision of your flesh, He has made alive together with Him, having forgiven you all trespasses, having wiped out the handwriting of requirements that was against us, which was contrary to us. And He has taken it out of the way, having nailed it to the cross. Having disarmed principalities [Satanic] and powers [demonic], He made a public spectacle of them, triumphing over them in it." (Colossians 2:13-15)

"Now may the God of peace who brought up our Lord Jesus from the dead, that great Shepherd of the sheep, through the blood of the everlasting covenant, make you complete in every good work to do His will, working in you what is well pleasing in His sight, through Jesus Christ, to whom be glory forever and ever. Amen." (Hebrews 13:20, 21)

Jesus has defeated the Devil, period!
The protection of the blood is YOURS;
take it and claim it.

God sent His Son, Jesus Christ, to pay the price for your salvation *and* your healing.

God loves you so much that He sent His Son, Jesus Christ, to restore
to you your health and to redeem you from all sickness.

However, Father God is more concerned with your spiritual healing
and wants to offer eternal life to you as well.

But just as you must make a choice to ask
and to trust Jesus Christ for your healing,
even so, you must ask Him for your salvation and eternal life.

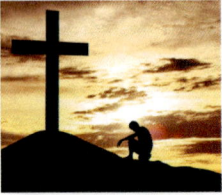

Again, the Choice Is Yours!

If you want to take the road toward Heaven that ends in eternal life,
you can do so by simply saying to Father God that you realize that you are a sinner,
ask Him to forgive you of your sins, and tell Him that you want to accept His Son,
Jesus Christ, as your Lord and Savior.
Then thank Father God for sending His Son into this world
for the express purpose of dying for your sins.

Your sins will then be removed as far as the East is from the West!

Ask Jesus to take control of your life from now
until He takes you home to be with Him.

Now Thank Jesus for What He Has Done for You!

Made in the USA
Monee, IL
16 October 2023

44693635R00031